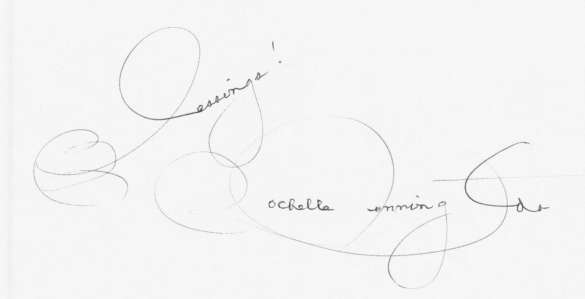

Blessings!

ochelle enning Ida

The ENDURANCE

Shackleton Family Shield
Dated 1779
Family motto: "By Endurance We Conquer"

The ⚜ENDURANCE⚜

History's Greatest Shipwreck

Rochelle Pennington and Nicholas Pennington

Published by Pathways Press

1-800-503-5507

All of the historic photographic images included in this book were used by permission of the following copyright holders with appreciation from the authors:
Royal Geographic Society, England
Scott Polar Research Institute, England
National Library of Australia

Grateful acknowledgment is further made to Tamara Thomsen and Keith Merveden, underwater archeologists from the State of Wisconsin, for photographing the underwater view of the ice used in *The Endurance*. A special thank you, also, to their assistant, Steve Smith.

The engraved image used on page 5 is by Elisha Kent Kane, as included in the book *Arctic Explorations*, published in 1856.

The authors extend appreciation to Deborah Simmons-Porter, Artist of Heraldry, for assisting with information regarding the Shackleton Family shield originally supplied by the Herald's Office in Dublin, Ireland.

Heartfelt gratitude to Linda Vis, Harold Reichert and Lucille Reichert for inspiring our project.
Your encouragement has guided us.

Rochelle wishes to thank her husband, Leslie, for all of his love and support over the past thirty years.
He is at the heart of everything she accomplishes.

Finally, the authors wish to extend a very special thank you to Sarah Vollmer-Griffin, Graphic Design Specialist at EP•Direct, as well as to her entire staff, for their tireless dedication to this project.

Printed in Canada

Pathways Press
1-800-503-5507
www.christmastreeshipbooks.com

ISBN: 978-0-9740810-3-8

The authors are available for lectures by calling 1-800-503-5507.

"Glittering white, shining blue...
in the light of the sun this land looks like a fairy tale."

Roald Amundsen

Dedicated to:

The Memory of Sir Ernest Henry Shackleton

"A True Descendant of The Sea Kings"

In memories we were rich... We had 'suffered, starved and triumphed'... We had seen God in his splendors, heard the text that Nature renders. We had reached the naked soul of man.

E.H.S.

We lived long dark days in the south.

The danger of the moment is in every man at some time. But I want to say to you that we lived through the slow dead days of toil, of struggle, dark striving and anxiety; days that called not for heroism in the bright light of day, but simply for dogged persistent endeavor to do what the soul said was right...

... Death is a very little thing – the smallest thing in the world. I can tell you that, for I have been face to face with death during long months. I know that death scarcely weighs in the scale against a man's appointed task.

Perhaps in the quiet hours of night, when you think over what I have said, you will feel the little snakes of doubt twisting in your heart. I have known them. Put them aside.

E.H.S.

The ENDURANCE

January, 1914. Frank Worsley sat up in an unfamiliar London bed, pondering the strange dream from which he just awoke. Worsley, a sea captain by profession, was momentarily taking stay in the port city until his next voyage was secured. As the mist of his sleep slowly receded into early-morning reality, Worsley grasped at the fading details of the fleeting dream. In his slumberland vision he had been awkwardly steering a ship down London's Burlington Street. If that hadn't been bizarre enough, there was the obstacle course of icebergs littering the ship's path.

Sailors of days past were notoriously superstitious, and to Captain Worsley, a life-long man of the water, the dream was not to be taken as mere coincidence. He replayed the events of the drama through his conscious mind while he quickly laced his boots and headed on foot to Burlington Street, hiking along the cobblestone route.

At first he felt a degree of certainty that his vision had beckoned within him a search for higher meaning, but after some time, with no sign or direction, he became foolishly aware of his wasted endeavor. Just before turning back, however, a small sign posted on a door, at the address of Number 4 Burlington Street, caught his eye. It read, "Imperial Trans-Antarctic Expedition." Strangely drawn to it, Worsley entered.

Inside the Burlington Street office were leaning stacks of letters, over five-thousand total, written in response to Sir Ernest Shackleton's curiosity-evoking expedition advertisement which warned, "Safe return doubtful." Applications and inquiries arrived from all corners of the globe, flooding the room by the bagful.

Shackleton's closest companion, Frank Wild, who served as second-in-command on the *Endurance,* helped sort through the long list of aspiring adventurers. Comparatively few were actually invited for a personal interview with Shackleton. These face-to-face meetings usually lasted only minutes, in which Sir Ernest made quick and final decisions for the makeup of his crew. His decisive abilities were hinged to an uncanny sense of character, by which he filled the ranks of the party. Among this carefully chosen entourage was an intricate mix of physicists, geologists, meteorologists, magneticians and medical doctors.

After long months of planning, funding and hiring, Shackleton delivered the eagerly-awaited announcement that the Imperial Trans-Antarctic Expedition, a complete on-foot crossing of the Antarctic Continent, would officially be undertaken by him and his crew, the bravest of the brave.

Queen Mother Alexandra of England, who three years prior had knighted Ernest Shackleton at Buckingham Palace for his earlier explorations, personally visited the ship in the London harbor before the vessel set sail. She arrived to offer her best wishes to

8

Sir Ernest Shackleton, Commander

members of the expedition and to present the crew with a Bible bearing an inscription written in her own penmanship: "May the Lord help you to do your duty and guide you through all the dangers by land and sea. May you see the works of the Lord and all his wonders in the deep." Queen Alexandra was thrilled at the opportunity to personally shake the hand of the expedition's famed leader, as well as the hand of the ship's captain, Frank Worsley.

Sixteen months later, under conditions of utter desperation, the treasured Bible would be laid down in the Antarctic snow. The only remnants of the priceless gift would be three pages carefully removed from the Bible's seam, folded neatly, and tucked safely into Shackleton's pocket. One page bore the Queen's inscription. Another was torn from the Book of Job and contained this verse: *"From whose womb comes the ice? Who gives birth to the frost from the heavens when the waters become hard as stone, when the surface of the deep is frozen?"* On the third page was printed the 23rd psalm, *"Yea, though I walk through the valley of the shadow of death, I will fear no evil, for thou art with me."*

If ever a man had been within an arm's reach of death, and managed to find his way out of the valley, it was Ernest Shackleton.

*   *   *

The goal of the expedition was to travel by wooden ship to the bottom of the world, where the icy and merciless sea swallowed whole those who attempted to trespass its jagged shores. A group of fearless adventurers, led by Shackleton, would cross the inner continent of Antarctica, from end to end, on foot, covering eighteen-hundred miles. The mission ultimately came to failure, but irrefutably became the most extraordinary journey of human strife and triumph that the pages of history have yet to reveal.

A leader among leaders, Shackleton himself detailed every aspect of the voyage. Each item to be packed was accounted for. With the precision of a mathematician he calculated amounts of food and supplies that he and his men would require to survive. All possible contingencies were carefully planned for – or almost all; but nothing could have prepared Shackleton for the twists of fate that were ahead in his future.

On August 1, 1914, the ship *Endurance,* carrying a crew of the most daring and courageous men of the time, departed the safety of the English shores simultaneous to the sudden outbreak of World War I in Europe. Three days later, England declared its entrance into the fight, and the patriotic group aboard the *Endurance* sent an immediate telegram back to their homeland offering their service at arms, as well as their sturdy ship, to the battle, fully ready to give up their hopes of Antarctic travel. Several of the men relinquished their opportunity for southern exploration and left the ship to join their comrades in the trenches. The others on board awaited a response.

The First Lord of the Admiralty, Winston Churchill, sent a one-word reply: "Proceed." And so they departed. As Shackleton tells of it, the crew ventured forward to its own battle, the "white warfare of the south." Having no contact with the outside world, worries and wonders of the war would become routine conversation among the men over the next two years. Under the extremities of their soon-to-be situation, comments were made alluding to thoughts that they would have fared safer in the war than stranded in the endless fields of ice.

Photographer Frank Hurley

Hurley, chosen by Shackleton to accompany the expedition, immortalized the events of the adventure *"which were so extreme that they would have strained credibility without the pictorial documentation."*

Hurley rescued the photographic glass plate negatives from the sinking ship:

"The negatives were located beneath four feet of mushy ice, and by stripping to the waist and diving under I hauled them out."

Frank Hurley

George E. Marston, crew member

Twenty-seven men remained aboard the *Endurance*, at least until a stowaway was discovered a short distance into the journey. The young man, Perce Blackboro, was found hidden below deck. Holding back a grin, Shackleton threatened the nineteen-year-old that the crew would be eating stowaways first if hunger were beset upon them. The brave young sailor was not swayed, and eyeing Shackleton's thick, muscular build, remarked, "They'd get a lot more meat off you, sir." Shackleton, nicknamed "The Boss" by those aboard the *Endurance*, admired Blackboro's courage and commented afterwards, "He will be an asset."

The *Endurance* and her crew proceeded forward, docking at a small whaling station on South Georgia Island, located beyond the lower tip of South America. This was the last outpost of humanity before entering the desolate, ice-strewn waters of Antarctica.

The station processed several whales daily, weighing up to 200 tons each. Whalers hunted these massive beasts using harpoon guns tipped with an explosive charge. In order to transport the slain whale back to the station, the blowhole was plugged and the creature was pumped full of air so it wouldn't sink to the bottom of the waters. The buoyant carcass was then floated back to the shoreline station. The remains of these giants were used to create such products as cooking oils, margarine and fuel for oil lamps. The Grytviken Whaling Station (pictured right) processed an estimated 174,000 whales during its operation.

As the ship approached the rocky shores, an odor, unlike anything imaginable, loomed heavy in the cold air. The remains of whales lay scattered on the beach, the carnage awaiting processing and shipment to merchant ports throughout the world. Here, on South Georgia Island, the ship was loaded with the remaining supplies needed to embark on this once-in-a-lifetime experience. The whalers, who spent much of their lives traveling the open waters, gave Shackleton a warning that the ice was the worst, and the farthest north, that any of them had encountered for that time of year.

On December 5, Shackleton and his band of thick-skinned explorers stood on the stony beach of South Georgia Island, then climbed aboard and raised anchor. This would be the last time their feet would be planted on solid ground for 497 days.

As the *Endurance* sailed south, forging forward toward the Antarctic continent, heavy ice – "the enemy" – was reached within two days, affirming the warnings given by the whalers. The sight of widening whiteness, extending unbroken to the horizon, did

ANTARCTIC WHALING

Types of whales processed on South Georgia Island:
Blue, sperm, humpback, orca ("killer whale") and fin.

Weight: Up to 400,000 pounds
(The tongue can weigh 22 tons.)

Length: Up to 110 feet

(The blue whale is the world's largest creature; it even surpasses the measurements of all dinosaur fossils found to date—including the brontosaurus.)

not sway Shackleton in his determination to reach and cross the icy outback, for "there seemed no reason to anticipate then that the fates would prove unkind," he recalled later.

The *Endurance,* a three-masted barkentine schooner constructed in Sandefjord, Norway, pressed forward. The vessel was the last of its kind to be built at the famous Framnaes shipyard which specialized in designing ships for polar travel, as well as whaling vessels. Being the grand finale of Framnaes' wooden-ship era, the *Endurance* received a sort of nostalgic nurturing in its crafting, as all of the workers bade farewell to the long-cherished art of hand-constructing Arctic vessels, now being replaced by steel.

The oak timbers used in the bow of the *Endurance* were each crafted from a single tree, hand-selected to match the grain of natural growth to the curve of the ship. In length, the ship stretched to 144 feet and boasted a 25-foot beam. The ship's maneuverability and sailing power were the result of three masts (the fore mast being square-rigged and the others being rigged with fore and aft sails), and the support of a 350-horsepower coal-fired steam engine. The original blueprints used to construct the *Endurance* are now housed at the National Maritime Museum in London. Frank Hurley referred to the vessel as "the bride of the sea," as it was the ship's maiden voyage; her first, and her last.

The vessel was reinforced with heavy oak beams and cased in greenheart, the densest timber on the planet, weighing more than solid iron. The wood was unable to be worked with standard tools. The hull of the ship was specially designed to withstand the impact of the blows it would receive as it plowed through large ice floes (huge flat pieces of ice floating on top of the water, much like rafts) surrounding the continent.

A man would be sent up into the "crow's nest" on the *Endurance,* the highest point, to scout out upcoming leads of open water between the ice floes. Then, from this perch, he would yell directions down to the men below indicating which path the ship was to follow through the crooked lanes. This slow and tedious work of "maneuvering to the south through the tortuous mazes of the pack" required continuous attention to the dangers the ice posed to the rudder and propeller, the most vulnerable parts of the ship. Collisions with the ice were a constant concern as the ship labored forward, threading its way through narrow open lanes, slowly advancing steadily south in its attempt to penetrate the polar wasteland.

Lacking the advanced technology of today's age, the navigation of the *Endurance* depended on a much more archaic, yet clever, means of choosing a suitable route. Called "ice-blink" the tactic entailed seeking out leads of open water using the reflection found on the underside of the clouds. If a cloud's coloring appeared dark, it indicated open water ahead, and was referred to as a "water-sky." If it was of a light color, or white, solid pack ice would be present ahead. At times, inconsistent stripes would be seen in the clouds, which told of open water leads between ice floes ahead. This proved to be a very useful navigational method; unfortunately, it could not be used on sunny days.

Into the sea of ice
December 9, 1914

"For three thousand miles, which included our turns and twistings, we fought our way through ice floes of every size, from a few yards across to great fields of two hundred square miles."

Captain Frank Worsley

ANTARCTICA

Average winter temperature: -40 to -94 degrees Fahrenheit
Average summer temperature: -5 to -31 degrees Fahrenheit
Coldest recorded temperature: -129 degrees Fahrenheit
Size: 7 million square miles (larger than the U.S. and Mexico combined)

    99% of the continent is covered in ice up to three miles thick. The continent doubles in size during the winter as the waters around it freeze solid at a rate of twenty-three square miles every minute. Winds can freeze exposed skin in seconds.

    Icebergs surrounding the continent ("wandering ice mountains") can be seen from the moon. The largest recorded iceberg measured 12,000 square miles, larger than the country of Belgium.

The *Endurance* zigzags through the maze

"We admire our sturdy little ship, which seems to take delight in combating our common enemy, shattering the ice floes in grand style. All day long we have been utilizing the ship as a battering ram... like a wedge... to enable a passage to be made."

Frank Hurley

On December 30, 1914, the *Endurance* crossed the Antarctic Circle, marking its entrance into "the worst portion of the worst sea in the world." It would take until the tenth of January before the white peaks of the sought-after continent were sighted.

Barely one week later, within a single day's journey of their destination, the *Endurance* and its crew became trapped in the rapidly forming ice. Thousands of ice floes, which Shackleton described as "a gigantic jigsaw puzzle devised by nature," drifted closer together, and pressed tighter and tighter around the ship, until the congestion made passage between the floes nearly impossible. Then, the sub-zero temperatures crept further downward, causing the water surrounding the floes to thicken into a mushy, "soupy" consistency.

"The character of the ice has changed," said Shackleton to Captain Worsley. "Yes," agreed the skipper. "It's like sailing into pudding."

The floes soon cemented together on all sides of the ill-fated *Endurance* and became one massive island of ice floating on top of the Southern Ocean with the ship firmly frozen in the middle. The *Endurance* came to a dead halt. The ship was stuck "like an almond in a chocolate bar," observed the ship's storekeeper. And there it remained.

Shackleton set the men to work on the task of breaking the imprisoned ship free of the vice-like grip using axes and picks. The men hacked away in their painstaking task and were able to remove several tons of ice from around the vessel, but in the extreme cold of the Antarctic, the ice reformed faster than it could be removed. Their efforts came to no avail.

"The actual cutting away of the ice with picks and saws is difficult enough," wrote crewmember Thomas Orde-Lees, "but lifting

"It is as though we are truly at the world's end, and bursting in on the birthplace of the clouds, and the nesting home of the four winds. One has the feeling that we mortals are being watched with a jealous eye by the forces of Nature."

Sir Ernest Shackleton

Splitting ice

Battling the ice

"We tried to cut away the ice to relieve the ship, but it was no use."
Harry McNeish diary
January 25, 1915

"All hands again attack the ice."
Frank Hurley diary
February 14, 1915

"If we do get jammed here for the winter we shall have the satisfaction of knowing that we did our darndest to try and get out."
Lionel Greenstreet diary
February 15, 1915

the blocks, some of which weigh as much as three and four hundred pounds, out of the water, hauling them away, breaking them up… entails much hard work."

Despite the men's determination to free the ship, the vessel remained gripped immovably, paralyzed in position, and would stay that way, until the warm, thawing temperatures of spring would arrive to free it.

The spring season, for which the men waited, would not begin until September, eight months away, because the seasons of the Northern and Southern Hemisphere occur opposite of one another. The lands of the north experience the warm glow of summer at the same time as the open Antarctic waters become frozen into winter ice. The *Endurance* was trapped in January, which meant that the whole and violent brunt of winter had not even begun to show its teeth.

Dr. Alexander Macklin noted in his journal, that when it became fully apparent that the entombed ship could not be removed from the ice, Shackleton showed one of his sparks of real greatness. "He did not rage at all, or show outwardly the slightest sign of disappointment," wrote Macklin. "He told us simply, and calmly, that we must winter in the pack ice, explained its dangers and possibilities, never lost his optimism, and prepared for winter." Despite their desperate situation, the stranded men, quite alone in their frozen world, remained fairly comfortable aboard

Attempting to free the imprisoned ship

"While unable to move within the tightly packed sea of ice, the
Endurance crew nonetheless hoped, and indeed initially expected, that the
winds and currents would eventually break up the ice pack, allowing them
to sail to freedom. When this expectation was not met, they resorted to
attempts to cut and saw the ship from the ice - puny, ineffectual attempts
that were mocked by the face of unconquerable nature."

Lord Mouser-Hunt

The doomed ship illuminated

Antarctica's winter season consists of approximately three months of complete darkness and is called "the long polar night." The summer season consists of approximately three months of complete sunshine.

"To the Sun," said Shackleton, lifting his mug, "whose light we will not see again for the next - how long is it, Hussey?"
"Seventy-nine days, sir," replied Leonard Hussey.
"To the Sun," said everyone.

the ship. Shackleton placed keeping the men in good spirits a top priority. He would not allow the depression that can accompany boredom to beset the men, so a daily routine was established. Each man was given responsibility over tasks that affected the wellbeing of the entire group. After all, even with the ship stuck in the ice, there was much that had to be done.

Shackleton retained his hopes that when their almond was released from the ice, the completion of the continental crossing would yet be possible. To ensure this, the sled-dogs on board required proper care and exercise. The animals were removed from their cages on deck and given their own area, which would come to be known as "dogtown." Dogtown was a swatch of ice next to the ship where small huts of snow served as shelters, nicknamed "dogloos" (instead of igloos), and provided a place for the dogs to rest and escape the cold winds. Men were assigned to feed and care for the dogs daily, which included regularly exercising all of the animals to keep them in shape for racing across the icy continent while harnessed to sleds loaded with gear.

Competitive feelings loomed between the commanders of each dog team. The men strived to offer their dogs the best training in order to out-drive the others. On June 15, an "Antarctic Derby" was held. All of the men cheered the drivers of each team as a competitive race over ice and snow ensued. Every man on board, Shackleton included, took part in the wagers that surrounded the event. Trapped in a world of snow and ice, with dwindling supplies, the "winnings" for the men crossing the finish line were the scarce commodities of chocolate and cigarettes.

Sailors were well-accustomed to the isolation aboard a ship (generally the ship would be sailing on open water), and were used to many forms of entertainment to retain their sanity. A variety of literature had been brought along and placed in the ship's library which helped to pass the time spent in quarters.

**Lead, kindly light,
amid the encircling gloom,
Lead Thou me on!**

**The night is dark,
and I am far from home,
Lead Thou me on!**

**Keep Thou my feet,
I do not ask to see
the distant scene;
one step is enough for me.**

Lead, Kindly Light
Shackleton's favorite hymn

"As we can expect no light from without, we must look for light from within."

Sir Ernest Shackleton

A moment's relief from the bitter cold

"From within the coziness of 'The Ritz,' it is hard to imagine we are drifting, frozen and solid in a sea of ice... I often wonder what is to become of it all."

Frank Hurley

The ship maintained a common room where the men gathered to eat their meals and play games - chess, cards and dominoes. They nicknamed this room "The Ritz," after the world-famous hotel in Paris, ironically symbolizing the height of luxurious living. Weekly theatrical events were hosted in which costumes were worn and music was played on crewmember Leonard Hussey's banjo. Other simple instruments brought along – a fiddle, a harmonica and a one-stringed violin – also aided in the merry-making. Shackleton made these events mandatory to keep morale high through the long winter months when darkness deepened.

"On one of these evenings," remembered Captain Worsley, "Shackleton cheerfully discussed taking an expedition to Alaska when the present journey was finished; so we looked up all the maps and books on the subject that we could lay our hands on and were enthusiastic about our next trip before we could definitely settle on how the devil we were going to get out of this one."

The men spent time outdoors playing hockey and soccer, as well as exploring nearby areas before the savagery of winter was upon them. On one such moonlit walk, Third Officer Alfred Cheetham remarked to Dr. Alexander Macklin who companioned him, "I say, Doctor, don't you think we are better off than the king?"

"I don't know, Cheetham," responded Dr. Macklin.

"Well, I'm happy, Doctor, and you're happy, and here we are sitting on a sled driving smoothly home (to the ship) and looking at the wonders of the world; it goes into your soul, doesn't it, Doctor? The king with all his might, and with all his power couldn't come here and enjoy what we're enjoying, for one thing he wouldn't be allowed to."

If the men aboard the ice-bound *Endurance* were going to survive the winter, as well as the voyage across Antarctica, food was an issue not to be overlooked. To manage their supply, and make their packaged stores last as long as possible, the men hunted penguins and seals. The meat from these animals is anti-scorbutic (scurvy preventing), and the blubber obtained from the flesh, especially from the 400-pound seals, was vital for fueling the cooking stoves.

On February 22, 1915, the *Endurance*, while still trapped in the ice, touched the 77th parallel. This would be the southernmost point reached during the journey. Since ice floes simply float on top of ocean waters, they can travel great lengths with the shifting currents and wind directions. Large storms and heavy gales can sometimes move these floes a distance of dozens of miles in a very short period of time.

Although the ship protected the crew from wind and storm, other dangers lurked as the men ventured out on the ice. "The floe was not so solid as it appeared," wrote Shackleton. "We had reminders occasionally that the greedy sea was very close, and that the floe was but a treacherous friend, which might open suddenly beneath us." This potentially catastrophic shifting of ice floes was one of several unseen hazards that existed silently beneath their feet. The fear of killer whales, which are generally not a direct predator of humans, also remained heavy on their minds. "These beasts have a habit of locating a resting seal by looking over the edge of a floe and then striking through the ice from below in search of a meal," wrote Shackleton in his journal.

Frank Wild, Second-in-Command

"They would not distinguish between seal and man." Occasionally, an emergence hole from a previous attack would be found during a walk along the ice, at times measuring wider than the height of two men combined.

The killer whale was not the only predator that lurked hungrily below the ice. Leopard seals, which can grow to a length of up to fifteen feet, could pose an even greater threat since they were capable of leaping from the waters and advancing on top the ice, awkwardly slithering their 1,000 pound bodies across the surface at speeds faster than a man could run – up to twenty-five miles per hour! The only commonalities between these beasts and actual leopards are "their spotted coats and their attitudes."

Thomas Orde-Lees nearly fell victim to one of these ferocious carnivores. He ventured a distance from the ship on skis when a sudden burst from below sent him on a panicked retreat. The deep snow on top of the ice slowed his escape, as the snarling predator closed its distance. In an attempt to confuse its prey, the clever sea leopard then made a dive into the open water and followed the man's shadow cast on the underside of the floe, only to resurface in an explosion of ice and water directly in front of the terrified skier. Luckily, the bloodcurdling screams from Orde-Lees' gasping breaths reached the keen ears of Frank Wild. Snatching up his rifle, and dropping to one knee, Wild took the beast down with a single shot – much to the relief of Orde-Lees.

Daylight was certainly unnerving at times, but then the darkness came.

"We said good-bye to the sun on May 1," wrote Shackleton, "and entered the period of twilight that would be followed by the darkness of midwinter."

A three month stretch of black frozen gloom – "the endless evening" – was now before them as winter approached. In Antarctica, the summer season brings three months of complete daylight to this far side of the world. The sun dips low in the sky, never quite setting below the horizon, but the winter season brings nearly three months of complete night when the continent is left in blackness. This three month span begins and ends with a few weeks of twilight. Such a continuous stretch of darkness would bear its weight on the psychological processes within the human body, causing severe depression and anxiety; not to mention the difficulties it posed to the men as they tried to perform simple activities.

Day passed day, and the ever-shortening hours of sunlight descended upon the crew, bringing with them increasingly colder temperatures.

The sea is frozen solid into a limitless expanse of ice

"All around us we have, day after day, the same unbroken whiteness, unrelieved by anything at all."

Dr. Alexander Macklin

Captain Worsley wrote, "Antarctic winter was setting in. Only those who have explored these regions can understand the full significance of this; for it means an unending series of blizzards, gales and blinding snowstorms, of pitiless winds that never give one a moment's respite, of seas that, save for brief intervals, grow continuously heavier and angrier, smashing the edges of the ice pack to fragments and splitting great bergs as though they were glass."

Doctor Macklin described the challenge of Antarctic weather in his diary also: "This place can be very nice when it wants to, but generally prefers to act like the devil."

Spring arrived in September, bringing with it strengthening daylight. Temperatures were on the rise as well. On September 10, 1915, the thermometer climbed to 1.9 degrees above zero – "the highest reading for seven months." It seemed like "a heat wave" to the men.

As the calendar turned from September to October, the ice floes which imprisoned the ship began to increase their grip with tremendous force, compressing the vessel's sides, squeezing the *Endurance*, and causing threatening leaks. Although the thousands of floes surrounding the ship were frozen into a solid cluster, the pressure from the raging sea caused the ice to shift and crack. Ribbon-like fractures appeared, snaking across the surface of the ice in all directions. These were called pressure ridges. As two floes were pushed against each other, one of the huge ice slabs was then lifted into the air and came to rest on top of the other floe, forming a cliff of ice which would commonly reach five to twenty feet in the air. These ridges then caught the pounding winds. The result was that the pressure of the pack was then multiplied, suffocating the weary vessel.

The ice, "like a volcano," was showing signs "of life." Captain Frank Worsley's diary noted, "Great spikes of ice were now forcing their way through the ship's sides." These stab wounds opened the *Endurance's* seams and allowed onrushing water to penetrate in. The men worked day and night, unceasingly, bailing water and trying to repair the leaky hull.

Shackleton set his crew to breaking up the ice surrounding the ship, and they hacked at it tirelessly. As a result of this, the ship actually floated free at one point in standing water. But millions of tons of pressure again moved closer and wrenched at the splintering wood of the *Endurance* once more, bludgeoning the vessel unceasingly, creating a devilish symphony of heartbreaking sounds. The *Endurance* began to "creak and groan like a haunted house." The ship, in its death struggle, cried out "like a living thing." The fearful noises remained in the memories of those on board years afterwards.

Harry McNeish, the ship's carpenter, recorded his first apprehension of the hostile advancement of the ice: "All hands standing by…. had a slight shock last night… there was a noise under the bottom… the Boss thinks it was a whale, but I think different." Shackleton would later describe the frightening, rumbling sounds heard from beneath:

"Standing on the stirring ice, one could imagine it was being disturbed by the breathing and tossing of a mighty giant below."

The buckling ice was now in continuous movement, heaving upward, and Captain Worsley attempted to describe the feelings of helplessness and unease among the men: "The night watchman reported that the ice ahead, along the port side, was on the move, but there was nothing the men could do, so they turned in; but a series of loud snapping noises, which reverberated throughout the ship, kept them awake most of the night. Those whose bunks were on the port side suffered the most. As they lay trying to sleep, they could hear the ice scraping against the hull outside – less than three feet from their ears…. Just after midnight there was a series of loud and violent cracks… making the ship jump and shake fore and aft. Many dressed hastily and rushed on deck. Personally, I got tired of alarms against which we could do absolutely nothing about, so when the loudest crash came, I listened to make sure that no ripping, tearing sound of smashing timbers was indicating an entrance of the ice into the hold, then turned over and went to sleep."

The *Endurance* keels over

"Then came that fateful day - Wednesday, October 27, 1915. The end of the Endurance *had come. It was a sickening sensation to feel the decks breaking up under one's feet, the great beams bending and then snapping with a noise like heavy gunfire."*

Sir Ernest Shackleton

"You could hear the ship being crushed up, the ice being ground into her, and you almost felt your own ribs were being crushed."

Lionel Greenstreet

The nervousness of the men increased with every broadside blow. "How long can this last?" wrote Leonard Hussey in his journal, "How long?"

The end was in sight, and everyone knew it. After long months of keeping the ice at bay, the *Endurance* was on the verge of succumbing to the pressure.

At this point, Shackleton sat down with Captain Worsley, just prior to the ship's demise, and tried to get a read on the skipper's feelings. Shackleton said to him in a "melancholy" tone, "Perhaps it's a pity, Skipper, that you dreamed a dream, or a nightmare, or whatever it was, that sent you to Burlington Street that morning we met."

"No," replied Worsley to Shackleton. "I've never regretted it, and never shall, even if we don't get through."

Shackleton was pleased. Lighting a cigarette, and walking away, Captain Worsley heard him murmur, "Good old, Skipper."

On October 27, the pressure grew too heavy for the beams to bear. Cracks in the ship widened and icy water filled the hull. Shackleton then gave the order, "Abandon ship."

Hurley noted in his diary that the last thing he looked at before taking his final leave was "the clock ticking on the wall." It was a strange sight.

Their faithful ship, now vacated, the only home the men had known in this frozen world "hidden away at the end of the earth," was crushed and destroyed before their staring eyes. The crew, almost 11,000 miles from England, was left "marooned" on their ice island with only five small tents, sleeping bags and three tiny lifeboats salvaged from the wrecked *Endurance*. "We were helpless intruders in a strange world," wrote Shackleton. "Our lives dependent upon the play of grim elementary forces that made a mock of our puny efforts."

No words can adequately describe the disparity and terror the men felt as each gazed upon endless miles of ice and snow, knowingly stranded, and realizing that no one was coming for them. They were alone.

As Alfred Lansing tells of it: "Nobody in the outside world knew they were in trouble, much less where they were. Thus, their plight was naked and terrifying in its simplicity. If they were to get out, they had to get themselves out."

Crushed "like an eggshell"

"The appearance of everything around us resembled the work of a hurricane. We were shipwrecked all right, but it was one odd looking shipwreck."

William Bakewell

Ice mask

Photographer Frank Hurley described the photo above: *"Our faces would mask with ice, through which we breathed with difficulty - and which we removed with painful care."*

Dr. Macklin, one of the ship's surgeons, recalled Shackleton's immediate reaction to the *Endurance's* final destruction after the vessel lost its battle with the elements: "As always with him, what had happened had happened; it was in the past and he looked to the future…. Without emotion, melodrama or excitement, he simply said, 'Ship and stores have gone, so now we'll go home.'"

If ever a leader held the respect of his crew, it was Sir Ernest Shackleton.

Second-in-Command Frank Wild noted that Shackleton had a "never-failing optimism, and the faculty of instilling the same into others." This skill would prove to be life-saving in the days and months ahead. Every single member of the twenty-eight man crew, standing on the ice, staring at their crumpled ship, would be tried to the fullest extent of human endurance, and Shackleton believed "an ordered mind" would be "essential" for survival.

Photographer Frank Hurley noted of Shackleton, "I always found him rising to his best and inspiring confidence when things were at their blackest."

Things were now very black indeed. Shackleton's goal of crossing the continent had been shattered. But instead of railing against the fates, he simply traded one objective

"It looked as if Father Neptune had poured out all his vengeance upon us for trespassing in his domains."

William Bakewell

for another. "If one goal has disappeared," reflected Shackleton, "then I will have another one. If I can't cross the continent, I will bring all my men back alive." This would prove to be a lofty task, beginning with the challenge of adequate shelter.

Far from the comfort the men had felt inside the once-sturdy walls of the ship, the crew now attempted to prepare a temporary campsite amidst the scattered supplies that were hurriedly thrown overboard when the hope of saving the *Endurance* had passed. This shambled mess of belongings, set against a background of splintered timbers, was quite an unsightly and depressing mess. The group coined the name of their new home "Dump Camp."

Shackleton was quick to realize the imperativeness of getting his men to land. It was uncertain how long they would survive on the open ice, vulnerable to nature's cruelest elements. Sir Ernest and his officers formulated a plan. After some contemplation, and knowing it was their only hope, Shackleton made the decision to embark on a 350-mile trek, across jagged ice and deep snow, toward Elephant Island. If fate was on their side, they could make it. Three lifeboats were then loaded with as much food and gear as each could hold, and harnesses were attached. The vessels weighed between two and four thousand pounds, and rested on sleds, awaiting transport.

To embark on such a crossing meant keeping the weight of each man's supplies at an absolute minimum. Shackleton gave the order to dispense of any non-essentials, and imposed a two-pound limit for personal items. He explained to the men, "The value of everything you carry must be weighed against your survival. Anything that cannot pull its weight, or is not useful to the expedition, must be put down." In his usual lead-by-example style, he tore three pages from the Queen's Bible and laid the book in the snow. After such a powerful gesture, the other men felt compelled to follow suit. To this order, Shackleton made few exceptions; a curious one being Leonard Hussey's twelve-pound banjo. "It's rather heavy. Do you think we ought to take it?" inquired Hussey. "Yes, certainly," was Sir Ernest's firm response. "It's vital mental medicine, and we shall need it."

The emotionally-strained men walked away from their personal items piled high; some of which were solid gold. "There are times," observed Captain Worsley, "when gold can be a liability instead of an asset." This was one of those times.

Trudging through snow, the men hauled one boat at a time a short distance forward, approximately one-quarter of a mile, and then returned for the second boat. Shackleton, accompanied by a few of his key officers, traveled by dogsled two miles ahead to scout out and clear a path for the boats to follow. It proved hellish work to weave through the gauntlet of pressure ridges and gaping crevasses. The men swung picks and shovels to dismantle the smaller ridges, hewing a flat, smooth surface for the boats to be dragged over. This strain along the rutted way exhausted their energy, but was, unfortunately, very necessary.

The men planned to travel as far as the solid ice would allow before making the final leg of the journey by open water, with the hope of landing on the shores of Elephant Island. Reaching the edge of the ice, with the boats undamaged, was their only chance of survival. This task was grueling, and drained the life from the men. Progress was excruciatingly slow; the average distance traversed was a mere mile per day. The sweat of the men's efforts saturated their clothing, then froze solid.

After three days of this back-breaking labor, the twenty-eight men were near exhaustion and Shackleton discarded the plan to trek on foot. He realized that it would take a year's worth of these slaving days to reach Elephant Island at this pace.

The frozen ice the men marched across was drifting with the ocean currents beneath; actually advancing on its own. This made it possible for their ice floe to be carried northward, nearer to Elephant Island, and hopefully within range of open water so the men could make an attempt at launching the boats.

Hungry, tired and barely three miles from the scraps of wood they once called *Endurance*, the group erected their tents and named their new home "Ocean Camp." Shackleton and his men would endure seven weeks at this village of tattered shelters. The wide-open ice provided little refuge from the battering winds which swept through the camp and chilled each man to the marrow of his bones.

November 7, 1915. Frank Hurley's diary reads, "It is beyond conception, even to us, that we are dwelling on a colossal ice raft, with but five feet of ice separating us from 2,000 fathoms of ocean and drifting along under the caprices of wind and tides to heaven knows where!"

Shackleton organized a team of men and sent them back to the wreckage site to retrieve supplies which had been abandoned. The group returned, bringing with them wood from the broken ship to craft planked floors for underneath tents in order that the men could once again sleep on a dry surface. (Their body heat melted the frozen floe beneath them as they slept. Pools of water accumulated below the slumbering men, saturating their sleeping bags.) The simple luxury of dry, wooden floors lifted spirits throughout the camp. Pieces of scrap metal were also retrieved and later fastened together to craft a small stove, fueled by seal and penguin blubber, on which the crew cooked their food.

Not long afterwards, on November 21, 1915, the *Endurance* disappeared into the icy depths, consumed by the waters below it. Although the ship was crushed beyond hope and abandoned on October 27, it took nearly one month longer for the fragmented remains of the rubbled shell to disappear completely.

In search of open water

Three salvaged lifeboats from the *Endurance* were dragged across the icy terrain by the men who *"strained forward, at times nearly parallel with the ground."* Each vessel was loaded with 2,000 - 4,000 pounds of supplies and gear.

The *Endurance*, padlocked in place for almost eleven months, from January until November, remained a familiar sight to the crew after it was vacated – even though it no longer served a useful purpose. The ship was their last symbol of the outside world in the midst of unending whiteness.

A wave of depression washed over the camp when the floes surrounding the mutilated *Endurance* parted wide enough to allow the greedy sea to swallow it. "Plank after plank disappeared under the ice," and the ship's remaining mast snapped off like a just-cut tree. It took only ten minutes for the vessel to vanish, and only one minute for

Preparing dinner for twenty-eight men

"Our food gets cold in our pots before we have eaten half of it, and the water we have brought in to drink becomes instantaneously covered with ice."

Captain Frank Worsley

the water above it to freeze over into a thickening skin of ice, mending the seam.

Shackleton's diary entry for the date is uncharacteristically brief. He simply noted that the ship had been lost, and added: "I cannot write about it."

December, 1915. Captain Worsley's calculations showed little progress made in the crew's drift toward Elephant Island, so Shackleton, running out of options, decided to make another desperate attempt at crossing the ice on foot.

The men re-fastened harnesses to two of the three lifeboats, the *James Caird* and the *Dudley Docker,* and prepared to set out. The smallest of the three, the *Stancomb Wills,* was left behind at Ocean Camp, as it was the least seaworthy of the vessels. (Each of the lifeboats was named after a major benefactor of the expedition.)

34

Just prior to vacating Ocean Camp, Shackleton sealed a note inside an empty pickle jar and left it there. The note read, "*Endurance* crushed and abandoned… All hands tomorrow proceeding to the westward. All well. December 23, 1915. E.H. Shackleton." The message was placed out of the sight of his crew because Shackleton feared the men would misinterpret the note as a sign that their leader was losing hope.

The twenty-eight labored forward across the trackless snow, hauling the two vessels loaded with gear, in the same manner as done before. Less than ten miles into the brutal trek, Shackleton, looking at the audience of strained faces before him, knew the group could stand no more. So, at this spot of unbearable exhaustion, the tents were pitched again. Their new home, "Patience Camp," was established. The name "Patience" was chosen because every man was acutely aware of the fact that the only thing left to do was wait; wait for the ice to carry them to Elephant Island, wait for open water to launch their boats, wait for the dwindling food to run out.

Survival depended on the presence of seals and penguins to subsidize the food supply, and with the Antarctic autumn approaching, the migration of these animals would make it exceedingly difficult to provide nourishment for twenty-eight starving men. Taking this into consideration, rations were cut to a bare minimum; just enough to sustain life. Hunger was constant, and the only consolation was that their misery was shared.

Shackleton then ordered the remainder of the dogs shot and used for food because the men were no longer able to spare enough of their own precious supply to feed the poor animals. He also ordered a return trip to Ocean Camp to gather any food stores which may have been left there, and to retrieve the *Stancomb Wills* vessel. Shackleton and his key officers believed that the entire twenty-eight man party would not fit in two boats.

Arriving at their former camp, the starving men found a can of cauliflower, a can of beets, a few baked beans and some dog food. The mixture was thrown into an empty metal gasoline container and cooked immediately. Dr. Alexander Macklin observed that the concoction was "very good," and Reginald James, the ship's physicist, called the meal "a great success."

The trip to Ocean Camp was made in the nick of time. Just after returning to Patience Camp with the precious boat, several serious cracks split the ice on the same evening and made travel back to Ocean Camp impossible.

Day passed day, and time dragged on. Shackleton's diary entries for January 26, 1916 and February 1, 1916 summarize their situation. The first reads: "Waiting, waiting, waiting." The second reads, "Patience, patience, patience."

The men continued to hunt for whatever food could be found. Their most clever hunting tactic was to stand on the edge of the ice and pretend to be penguins, hopping

up and down, bouncing from side to side with arms stiffened, mimicking the movement of a sea leopard's favorite meal in order to lure the gigantic beasts out of the water. Once on the ice, the 1,000 pound creatures could be shot, and the food supply lavishly replenished.

The floe supporting Patience Camp finally began to crack and break as huge chunks of ice were ripped from its edges. This "island" beneath the camp was becoming smaller and smaller, and was now influenced by the heavy swells from the pulsating ocean below. The floe bobbed several feet into the air as the sea rolled beneath. Shackleton described the solid mass under their feet as "but a sheet of ice floating on unfathomed seas."

As their slab was further reduced, only a fifty-yard span remained between its edges. Surrounded by thousands of other rafts of ice, the men watched helplessly as their home was raised upward on the crest of each new wave, and then dropped a moment later into a trough walled by twelve-foot swells. It was a terrifying sight.

The men waited for the mosaic of ice floes to separate enough to allow water to widen between them, making it possible for the boats to be safely launched. Each vessel was loaded with gear so it would be ready in a moment's notice.

The camp quivered from whales rubbing against the ice from below. Every man realized the frozen floe beneath them, now greatly reduced in size, could be flipped over by the onrushing swells of water, or by a surfacing whale. Alert to this possibility, the men feared their capsizing floe would fling them into the sea, and to certain death.

As the ice floes collided continuously with each other, a tremendous blow split their camp in two. On one side of the crack were the men; on the other side were the boats. Through rapid efforts, several crew members jumped across and retrieved the vessels, reuniting them with the camp. Then, the men leapt back, one by one. Shackleton had yet to make the leap. He waited for the others to cross first before making his move, but suddenly found himself alone on the deserted floe with the slabs separating further. Unable to negotiate the gap, Shackleton floated away into the dark of the moonless night on the drifting floe. His comrades hurriedly launched a boat and wove between the sharpened edges of the surrounding ice in search of the isolated Shackleton. Following only the sound of his voice, at last they came upon him.

Despite this near catastrophe, it still was not safe for the men to abandon their floe. The risk of launching the boats was far too great. The frail vessels would almost certainly be crushed in the narrow water-lanes of the shifting, congested ice.

The men, restless and impatient, waited for a clearing. It was now April, the fifth month of living on the ice, and another near-fatal mishap occurred. It happened, again, in the night. The floe split in two, but this time the crack opened beneath one of the tents, tearing it in half. Most of the men were able to escape from under the shredding canvas.

Danger lurked beneath the ice

"No man could sleep at night and expect to wake safe in the morning."
Captain Frank Worsley

One man, however, Ernest Holness, had been sleeping directly above the crack and fell straight down into the opening. He was trapped inside his sleeping bag, "wiggling like a worm" in the icy water, frantically trying to free himself. Shackleton rushed to the edge of the split and, reaching down, seized the submerged man with a single arm. Holness, still cocooned in his heavy, sopping bag, was hoisted to safety, snatched back

Ice floes at a pressure ridge

"The blizzards seemed unending, and the ice floes appeared to us to be alive, fighting each other, hurling against one another, and uniting only to attack."

Captain Frank Worsley

from death, by Sir Ernest. The ice slammed shut again with a million tons of pressure barely ten seconds later, "like the jaws of a snapping trap."

Enough was enough. The men knew they had to get off the floe. No one slept for the remainder of that night, and the next morning Shackleton gave the order to launch the boats. It was April 9, 1916. None of the men wanted to stay on the disintegrating floe for even a moment longer.

The men cautiously steered each vessel through a maze of jagged, sharp-edged floes. A single mistake could have sent a spear-like protrusion of ragged ice through the thin planks of the boats, creating a gush of frigid water.

After long hours of tedious maneuvers, the men were finally able to escape the closeness of the ice pack. This brought them no added safety; only a change in the desolate scenery.

The biting Antarctic winds caught the tips of waves and cast a salty spray sixty feet into the air. Showering down, it then crystallized, coating both crew and boats in a frozen "icy armor." The men became covered in massive saltwater boils which broke open and bled, making rowing an exercise in excruciating pain. Captain Worsley observed that their flesh "assumed a dead-white color and lost surface feeling" during the seven-day boat journey due to the "constant soaking in seawater." The Antarctic cold also repeatedly caused the men's eyes to form tears. Alfred Lansing observed that these then "ran down a man's nose and formed an icicle on the end, which sooner or later had to be broken off. No matter how carefully it was done, a patch of skin invariably came off with it, leaving a chronically unhealed sore on the end of his nose."

Most of the men caught little sleep during the final four days in the open boats, and some didn't sleep at all. Captain Worsley again noted, "During one-hundred hours of hardship and exposure, Shackleton and Wild had not slept. Greenstreet and I each slept for about an hour."

The waves crashed continuously over the sides of the boats, slapping each man across his face. The men, achingly cold, bailed furiously, some even using their cupped hands to ladle the intruding waters overboard.

Escape from the ice; a seven day journey in open boats

"We were cold, wet, hungry, thirsty and disappointed. The night was everything that represented misery."

William Bakewell

Breath icicles

First officer Lionel Greenstreet, in the photo above, lived to be 89 years old. He was interviewed at 82 and asked, *"How did you survive in Antarctica when so many expeditions failed?"*

Greenstreet responded in one word: *"Shackleton."*

"Pull your damnedest!" was the repeated order, as the men fought their way through the vile weather and iron seas.

Crashing waves blanketed all three vessels in ice, weighing them down. Oars froze to the boats, and hands froze to the oars.

In order to steer through the wild waters, the men on board took turns watching for incoming waves. This task required that a watchman was perched on top of crates and supplies. On the *James Caird*, Shackleton took his turn to watch, and remained in position for such an extended period that the circulation was chilled from his body. He was literally frozen into place, statue-like, iced over, and needed to be chipped free. Then, his fellow crewmembers "straightened him out like a jack-knife," massaging feeling back into his limbs until he was able to move again, unassisted.

"It is very hard to imagine, but when we finished our turn rowing the boats, our hands were blocks of ice and actually had to be chipped off the oars."

Peter Wordie

As the journey progressed, Captain Worsley took a calculation of the distance traveled. He, as well as Shackleton, estimated a gain of approximately thirty miles, but the measurement proved to the contrary. Worsley, speaking under his breath, informed Sir Ernest that the current had actually carried them nearly thirty miles in reverse. Their efforts had been futile; they were losing ground instead of gaining it. Shackleton, not wanting to kill the spirit of hope within his exhausted men, simply stated, "We haven't done as well as we expected." (Shackleton knew it was imperative for his men to keep their minds as positive as possible in order to endure the trials that were yet to come.)

Whales surrounded the vessels as they travelled, their hissing noises frightening the men, especially at night. "The slow, measured rising of the white-throated whales in the dark waters around their boats," wrote Caroline Alexander after reading crewmember diaries, "remained one of the most terrible and abiding memories the men would carry with them. In their long months on the ice, the men had bourn abundant witness to the great beasts' ice-shattering power."

After nearly a week in the boats, the need for drinking water consumed their every thought. The men had abandoned the crumbling Patience Camp in such a panicked hurry that they forgot to load blocks of ice, which, melted down, would provide them with fresh water. (Due to the heavy content of salt found in seawater, consuming it causes severe dehydration which leads to death because the kidneys are unable to process the salt. Ice from the Antarctic continent, or from ice hummocks, held fresh water, as the saltier waters around these would only freeze at a much colder temperature.) To quench their miserable, choking thirst, the men chewed bits of raw seal meat just to feel the sweet moisture of the blood trickle down their swollen, parched throats. Shackleton noted, "The only dry things aboard the boats were swollen mouths and burning tongues."

When it seemed as if the men could endure no more, the glorious sight of land was spotted on the distant horizon. Shackleton felt a surge of relief when the peaks of Elephant Island came into view. He admitted later that he seriously doubted as to whether all of his men would survive the last night of the journey since some of them were weeping without trying to stop, some were cursing, and still others remained strangely silent, their voices seemingly frozen, their motionless eyes staring. Shackleton recalled, also, how he repeated the words of the poet, Coleridge, to himself in the final hours of the journey: "Alone, alone, all all alone, alone on a wide, wide sea."

Finally, the three worn vessels came to rest on the shore. The men leapt from the boats as if their battered, wooden hulls had suddenly caught fire. Then, they ran wildly to and fro on the beach. It was the first time their feet were on land - "solid, unsinkable, immovable, blessed land" - in nearly a year and a half. Shackleton noted that the men were "laughing uproariously, picking up stones and letting handfuls of pebbles trickle between their fingers like misers gloating over hoarded gold."

Although whaling ships and other explorers had sighted Elephant Island in the past, none had yet ventured onto its shores. Shackleton, who had acquired a soft spot for the young stowaway, Perce Blackboro, helped the frostbitten lad out of the boat so that he would receive the honor of being the first man in history to plant his tethered sole on the frozen ground of this desolate land. (Blackboro's toes were later surgically amputated on Elephant Island by the ship's surgeons after they discovered the flesh had peeled back, and turned completely black, ironically as if it had been burned.)

The crew found two seals casually lounging on the beach upon their arrival, almost as if someone knew they would be starving and in desperate need of food. The animals were immediately killed, and their meat created a fine feast, well-deserved.

With their feet planted firmly on dry land, the men were finally free from their icy prison. Shackleton had chosen these warriors well; each had forged forward and displayed remarkable determination. "As we clustered around the blubber stove on Elephant Island, with the smoke blowing into our faces," wrote Shackleton in a tired hand, "we were quite a cheerful company. After all, another stage of the homeward journey had been accomplished, and we could afford to forget for an hour the problems of the future."

As wonderful as they felt to be huddled together on the far-from-comfortable, rocky shores of the island, their safety, again, was an illusion. Shackleton, eyeing the water marks high on the cliffs surrounding their small beach, knew that a tide could swoop in at any moment and wash them helplessly out to sea. He decided, however, to allow the crew to remain on the beach for the night because the men badly needed rest. But when morning came, he knew he would be compelled to give the heart-wrenching order to climb back into the boats.

The following day, the men, again, took to the boats, traveling through the surging ocean they had been freed from only one night before. Seven miles down the shore, they found a small, secure cape at which they made camp. This new beach seemed free from immediate dangers. (By "free from immediate dangers" it is meant only that the ground beneath them was not going to crack open and pull them to the bottom of the sea, killer whales would not be eating them for dinner, a gale was not going to pursue them relentlessly when their only shelter was a lifeboat, and they were not going to be literally dying of thirst in the midst of water everywhere.)

The men were safe for the moment, but this was certainly no paradise. Their new home was comprised only of barren rock and ice, void of any vegetation. There were, however, enough seals and penguins to feed their hungry mouths for the time being, and so they proceeded to eat and sleep, and eat again, and sleep some more.

For the first few days, the men could only bring their weary bodies to accomplish the repetition of resting and eating, nothing more. It would take many more days for the group to fully recover from the exhaustion induced by the horrific week in the boats.

Shackleton was well aware that this new-found sense of security would not last. He also knew what must be done. On April 20, he announced to the men that he would

Landing on Elephant Island
April 15, 1916

"Such a wild and inhospitable coast I have never beheld... 'A land of savage grandeur that measures each man at his worth.' "

Frank Hurley

be making an attempt for South Georgia Island, 800 miles distant, in the *James Caird*, the largest and strongest of the three lifeboats. Shackleton then asked for volunteers. Nearly every man stepped forward, willing to accompany him on the dangerous quest. Shackleton voiced his gratitude with three simple words: "Thank you, men."

Frank Wild, second-in-command, and Sir Ernest's closest friend, begged to join him on the voyage, but Shackleton asked that he remain on Elephant Island to assume leadership of the remaining twenty-two. Wild was given written instructions to do all in his power to save the remainder of the crew if the rescue attempt to reach South Georgia Island fell to failure.

The next few days were spent preparing the boat for the perilous journey. The three ice-gourged lifeboats had barely survived the voyage to Elephant Island, and the far-from-seaworthy *James Caird* would now face another unthinkable stretch of impossible travel through the most treacherous waters in the world.

The ship's carpenter, Harry McNeish, removed extra wood from the remaining two boats and raised the sides of the *James Caird* to protect its passengers from the battering waves that would toss endlessly. He also covered the shell of the vessel with a thin decking, placing a few boards for support, then covering them with canvas sewn from scraps of shredded tents. This would, at the very least, give the six a crude shelter from the heavy winds and icy sprays, which stung "like sharp pins on bare flesh." The rowboat was also fitted with make-shift sails.

The vessel was stocked with adequate food and water to keep the six alive for thirty days. Shackleton, with the help of Worsley, his trusted navigator, estimated that it would not take longer than this to reach South Georgia; and if it did, they would not survive long after in the rickety boat anyway.

On April 24, 1916, six men – Ernest Shackleton, Frank Worsley, Thomas Crean, Harry McNeish, Timothy McCarthy and John Vincent – set sail in the *James Caird*, bound for South Georgia Island. With one glance backward, they waved goodbye to the twenty-two left standing on the shores, fully aware that seeing them again was not likely. Shackleton reflected, "They waved to us and gave three hearty cheers. There was hope in their hearts, and they trusted us to bring the help they needed."

Crossing the fierce waters of the Southern Ocean was a suicide mission, but it was their only chance of survival. No one was coming for them, and they knew it. No ships would be sailing past to spot a signal fire. No daring rescue party was being organized.

Ice cliffs

"It is a unique sort of feeling to look at lands that have never been seen by the human eye before."

Sir Ernest Shackleton

Launching the *James Caird*, their last chance for rescue
April 24, 1916

Shackleton and a crew of five attempted to reach civilization, 800 miles away, in the largest of the three lifeboats. Frank Wild was appointed commander of the twenty-two men left behind on Elephant Island, per the correspondence below:

April 23, 1916
Dear Sir,

In the event of my not surviving the boat journey to South Georgia Island, you will do your best to rescue the party. You are in full command from the time the boat leaves this island, and all hands are under your orders... I have every confidence in you, and always had. May God prosper you and your life. You can convey my love to my people, and say I tried my best.

Yours sincerely,
Ernest Shackleton

The men aboard the *James Caird*, huddled in the crawl space of the shallow boat, were the last hope of the expedition. The twenty-two who remained to struggle on peered out at the bobbing vessel until it finally vanished beyond the curve of the earth, lost to sight.

The *James Caird*, only six feet wide, the width of a grown man's outstretched arms, proceeded into the stormy turmoil of the surrounding ocean. The canvas deck helped to block the biting spray of the wind-swept waves, but leaks poured constantly down on the men crunched below, soaking everything in the boat, including their clothing and sleeping bags. Life inside this rocking shelter was beyond miserable. Water had to be bailed non-stop. The crew, soaked through, divided the task of bailing, as well as other duties on board, between three men who worked in four hour shifts each. This allowed the other three to make a feeble attempt at resting.

"We watched them until they were out of sight, which was not long, for such a tiny boat was soon lost to sight on the great heaving ocean. As the boat dipped into each wave, it disappeared completely, sail and all."

Thomas Orde-Lees

Due to months of saturation, the reindeer sleeping bags were now molting and smelled of spoiled meat. The hairs from the putrid, slimy bags separated from the hides and covered everything – their bodies, their faces, their food and their water. The hairs stuck to the inside of their mouths like peanut butter.

There was no comfort below the deck of their tightly-cramped vessel. Two tons of rocks lined the bottom of the boat and served as ballast (weighing the boat down in the water so that the massive waves would not toss it about like a piece of driftwood). Because of the rocks, there wasn't enough room for the men to sit erect, and the crew had to eat lying nearly flat, resting on their sides, supported by an elbow painfully positioned on top the jagged pile. (If the men tried to sit upright, their chins would press against their chest, making swallowing impossible.) The crewmembers entertained their imaginations by pretending they were reclining Roman Emperors, lounging at an eloquent feast. This helped to take their minds far from the miseries of their reality, but day after grueling day, their bodies grew weary of being positioned in abnormal postures while living on top their stony mattress.

The men worked in darkness beneath the deck with only a minimum amount of daylight penetrating through the opening in the deck floor. One small "stump" of a candle was lit sparingly, providing vision enough to cook meals by, or to read a critical navigation map.

Below the shoddy deck, the men clumsily groped their way through the darkness, crawling on all fours. Their wet clothing chaffed their flesh raw. In addition, all of the men were frostbitten severely. Huge blisters formed on their hands and fingers where patches of flesh had been eaten away.

Colossal waves continued to bash the canvas decking, and the water began to freeze. Then, a thin layer of ice formed on the topside of the boat. Because of this, the dripping waters (which had been "raining" down on them since the voyage commenced) suddenly ceased. The halted leaking was looked upon as a strange "miracle." However, the ice on the outside of the boat soon grew to "the width of a man's thigh," and weighed the boat down dangerously, threatening to capsize it. Their miracle had been quickly transformed into a curse. The men needed to remove the ice, and remove it immediately. Each man, in his turn, crawled out of the boat's sheltered depth and climbed onto the slippery surface outside, then attempted to club away at the icy buildup. As Captain Worsley told it: "We took turns and crawled out with an axe to chop off the ice. What a job! The boat leaped and kicked like a mad mule…. First you chopped a handhold, then a knee hold, and then chopped off ice hastily, but carefully, with an occasional sea washing over you. After four or five minutes – fed up or frostbitten – you slid back into the shelter, and the next person took up the work… If a man had gone overboard, it would have been goodbye… This fierce, cold gale lasted for forty-eight hours. During that period we had, no fewer than three times – once practically in the dark – to crawl out on top of the boat to chop and scrape the ice off."

On a morning with skies shadowed by relentless storms, Shackleton was gazing toward the horizon when he caught sight of what looked like a parting in the gray skies, a patch of whiteness. Overjoyed at this heavenly sign that the storm was nearing an end, he called the good news out to the others below. Taking a second glance, however, he saw that it was not a clearing after all. Instead, the white coloring was actually the crest of a giant "rouge" wave, similar to a tidal wave – careening directly toward them. Sailors refer to this terrifying phenomenon as "the white manes of the galloping horses." Captain Worsley, writing his memories of the experience, noted that he feared that "the white horses of the hurricane, whose pounding hooves we felt" would smash their frail craft. Shackleton shouted, "For God's sake, hold on! It's got us!" The enormous wave came crashing over the *Caird*, nearly submerging it permanently.

When the tumbling and twisting subsided, the crew found their vessel half full of icy water. The men bailed with all speed, and the craft broke free, once again, of the sea's turbulent grip.

Shackleton was a sailor with twenty-six years of experience under his belt, many of these years spent sailing on the most vicious waters on the globe. He observed, without exaggeration, that this wave was, beyond a doubt, the largest he had ever laid eyes on; and they had survived it… in a lifeboat.

After reaching the halfway point of the voyage between the islands, the men on board recalled the sailor's adage, "What we have already done, we can do again!" Then, they pressed onward.

Nearing the journey's end, the men noticed a crack in one of their water jugs. Because of this, some of their precious supply was contaminated with saltwater and had to be relinquished. Worsley calculated the distance remaining as being still several days from reaching the destination of South Georgia Island. This was bad news with the water now running dangerously low. So, Shackleton drastically reduced the water rations to a mere half cup per day per man in order to preserve it until their voyage ended. The men sometimes begged him to grant them even a swallow, but Shackleton remained steadfast in his decision; he knew he must, or all would die.

Nearing noon on May 8, fourteen days after their departure from Elephant Island, McCarthy, barely able to contain his excitement, proclaimed a glimpse of land spotted between the passing clouds. The others frantically crawled over the rocks and rushed to the opening in the decking. For a brief moment, they saw what looked like a snow-capped peak far into the distance. But the cloudy skies quickly reformed, masking the view. Unsure if the vision had actually been land, or just fatigue and delirium playing cruel games with their senses, the group glued their widened eyes to the horizon, awaiting another sign. Finally, the cloud cover dissolved and the men beheld a sight even more glorious than Elephant Island. They were approaching the long-awaited, and well-deserved, shores of South Georgia Island; the end was near. Now, for the first time in many months, they knew—not hoped—they could make it.

Captain Frank Worsley, "The Skipper"

"The boat behaved like a thing possessed. It staggered drunkenly upward over each new wave, then plunged sideways only to have its bow jerked violently around... There was never a moment, not even an instant, of repose. The only thing to do was to hang on, and endure."

Alfred Lansing

It must be noted that this 800-mile passage could not have been accomplished successfully without the wondrous navigational skills of Captain Worsley. Using only a sexton (a small triangular tool to measure the angle of the sun), a book of maps, a compass, and a chronographer (an accurate time piece used in primitive boat travel), the skipper piloted them across the most feared ocean in the world with exacting calculations to the safety of South Georgia's rocky edge. It was the "navigational equivalent of finding a needle in a haystack."

By the time the crew made their final approach to the shores, Worsley noted, "My navigation books and log were in a pitiable state—soaked through, stuck together, illegible, and impossible to write in. The pages were not paper pulp, but something like it, and I needed to use great care to open them without completely destroying all chance of navigation to land." In the initial preparation of the expedition, twenty-four chronographers had been taken along, but only one of these remained—the instrument now used by Worsley. (The others had been broken during the course of their travels.) Without this priceless chronographer, it would have been impossible to accurately direct the *James Caird* to the "pinpoint" of South Georgia Island in the midst of the vast waters. The crew would have passed the island completely, never coming within sight of its shores.

The U.S. Navy's Sailing Directions for Antarctica describe the ceaseless gale-force winds found in this area of the ocean as follows: "The winds are often of hurricane intensity, with gust velocities sometimes attaining 150 to 200 miles per hour. Winds of such violence are not known elsewhere, except perhaps in a tropical cyclone."

According to Alfred Lansing, these latitudes, as no where else on earth, produce winds which mercilessly drive the seas clockwise around the earth to return again to their birthplace where they reinforce themselves or one another.

Waves in this region can routinely reach heights of fifty feet (and are estimated by scientists to reach upwards to ninety feet), pounding down on ships with a hundred-million tons of water. Charles Darwin, after seeing these monstrous walls of water, recorded in his diary: "The sight is enough to make a landsman dream for a week about death, peril and shipwreck."

The U.S. Navy's Sailing Directions for Antarctica also warns sailors about the danger of a "cross sea" – a condition created when the wind is blowing in one direction, and the current is moving in another.

The unmapped mountains of South Georgia Island

Captain James Cook discovered South Georgia Island in 1773. He described it as being *"a land doomed by nature to perpetual frigidity, a terrain savage and horrible... not a tree or a shrub to be seen, no, not even big enough to make a toothpick."*

"Look at a man in the midst of doubt and danger, and you will learn in his hour of adversity what he really is. It is then that true utterances are wrung from the recesses of his breast. The mask is torn off; the reality remains."

Lucretius

The weather turned against them as they closed in on the outskirts of the island. No suitable place to land could be found along the mammoth cliffs which dropped off vertically, straight down into the sea. The waters surrounding the island were scattered with underwater reefs, hanging just below the surface, reaching upward with razor-like fingers, grasping to pull the *Caird* to an icy grave. If the boat had not been steered with precision, the jutting rocks would have ripped out the bottom of the vessel.

Night was falling fast, and the exhausted men needed water desperately. However, there was no safe place to bring the boat ashore. Shackleton then made the decision to spend another grueling night at sea. The ocean, with renewed violence, gathered its mighty breath once more during the following morning and made its last stand, hurling a massive hurricane at the men. The formidable foe would not release the crew without a final fight. Shackleton and his five companions spent the day battling the winds and waves which opposed them, struggling to keep their little craft from being smashed to rubble against the jagged cliffs. Finally, as the long day neared its end, the combative temperament of their stubborn enemy began to calm. (This same storm sunk a 500-ton steamer near South Georgia Island. Every man on board perished.)

Thirst and exhaustion grew to an intensity, and Shackleton determined that a landing must be attempted the following day—at any risk. If they failed to land safely on the shores, it would be death, not dry land, soon arriving to free them from their suffering.

May 10, 1916 was a date that brought feelings of relief the men would not soon forget. Finally, after 800 miles and seventeen days, the goal was reached. The crew landed their weathered lifeboat on the shores of South Georgia, narrowly escaping the tangled dangers of the journey. Shackleton would later sum up the trial they suffered as "supreme strife amid heaving waters."

The six men wearily climbed from the boat and into the icy surf. Gathering around the sides of the vessel, the men heaved with all their remaining strength, trying to pull the *Caird* on shore; but their limbs failed them. They lacked the vigor to haul the boat from the mocking waters.

After this long and horrific journey, nearly dead from manual toil, the men, dehydrated and exhausted, were now left taking turns, standing unsheltered on the windswept beach, holding on to the ropes of the boat to keep it from being ripped back into the violent sea. The first shift was, of course, endured by Shackleton. Worsley recorded the miseries of this task: "Taking turns to watch the boat, we snatched such sleep as we could until two o'clock in the morning. Then Thomas Crean, who was hanging on to the rope, gave a shout. We all rushed out, and, stumbling in the darkness to him, found that a big sea had torn out the boulder to which the line was secured, and that Crean, hanging on to it, had been dragged into the waters which threatened to submerge him. We all held the rope together, and hauled the boat up to the beach again… There was no more sleep. All hands had to hold on to the boat for the rest of the night. When our spirits were almost down to zero, Shackleton got a laugh out of us by saying, with the most elegant formality, 'I do hope that you are all enjoying my little party.'"

Late the next day, with a bit of rest collected behind their drooping eyes, the men found the strength to tow the *Caird* up to safety. Then, the castaways continued to rest for several days in a cave, eating and sleeping long hours to regain the strength which had been stripped from them on their voyage.

They built a small fire using clumps of grass from the shoreline, as well as scraps of wood found on the beach where endless tides deposited the depressing remains of age-old shipwrecks. With this life-giving heat they were able to thaw their frozen bodies, bringing the sharp pains of recirculation. The six slept with numb, frostbitten feet close to the crackling flames during the first night. As life returned to their toes, and slowly moved upward, the men described feeling as if their feet were on fire. One night, while the men attempted to sleep, Worsley repeatedly shouted out, waking the others, claiming that he was certain his feet were engulfed in the flames, but he was too tired to raise himself up to check. His comrades assured him that they were all suffering the same pains as he was while feeling was being returned to their thawing limbs also. Waking in the morning, however, Worsley found his boots and socks burned through. Luckily, his feet were far too saturated to be wounded by the heat.

The cave sheltering them was on the opposite side of the island from the whaling station. Because of this, the men now faced the decision of how to proceed. The whaling camp lay 150 miles distant if the crew were to take the already-battered *James Caird* along the dangerous, reef-strewn outskirts of the shoreline. Shackleton doubted the vessel would survive another beating from the sea. Alternatively, the men could cross the island on foot, but this option would be desperately difficult since the interior of South Georgia was completely unmapped at that time and a crossing had never been attempted—even by the most experienced and well-equipped mountaineers of the time. The majority of the island was covered by a monstrous mountain range, nicknamed "The Alps of the South Ocean," with looming peaks reaching a height of nearly 10,000 feet. (A true island only by definition, South Georgia was merely an outcropping of rock; simply the unsubmerged tip of a colossal underwater mountain range.) The peaks on South Georgia were home to deep-gorged crevasses and 163 glaciers, with other variations of the most life-threatening terrain in the world, all cunningly hidden under blankets of drifted snow.

A man could take a seemingly harmless step forward onto what appeared to be solid landscape, and fall downward to his death through a concealed split in the ice.

Shackleton analyzed his options and, looking skyward, lingered his gaze on the summits, knowing that the only viable choice was to traverse the treacherous range.

On May 19, Shackleton, Worsley and Crean began their inland climb up the forbidding peaks, leaving the others who were physically unable to manage the slopes behind to wait for them.

The trio held no experience in mountain climbing—they were sailors. They possessed no gear, other than ice axes and a single rope salvaged from the *Caird* to assist them. They packed a small blubber stove on which to cook their three-day ration of food. Their clothing was ragged and worn thin; certainly not proper attire to protect them against the bone-chilling cold of the higher altitudes. Screws were driven through the soles of their boots, point down, to help create greater traction on the slippery, slanting surfaces, some of which were "as perpendicular as a church steeple," recalled Worsley.

The brave three said goodbye and headed upward, roped together. This was a precaution against a fatal tumble into a crevasse or a fall down a mountainside. Drawing hard breaths over the hardly-manageable and hazardous landscape, they pressed onward in rapid ascent over rock and cliff.

The mountains seemed unending, stretching north, south, east and west; in every direction, it was all the same. The men were quickly exhausted and in dire need of rest. Worsley and Crean begged Shackleton to grant them thirty minutes of sleep to relieve their heavy eyes. Shackleton knew the dangers of falling asleep in such low temperatures, and understood that the unconscious body would perceive the increasing cold as warmth. Then, as the comfortable snooze continued "in the embrace of the Frost King," the painless death from freezing would occur. Shackleton agreed to their request, but stayed awake himself. "It would have been disastrous if we had all slumbered together," wrote Shackleton, "for sleep under such conditions merges into death. After five minutes I shook them into consciousness, told them they had been asleep for half an hour, and gave the word for a fresh start."

Death was close, as near as their own breaths, and would have been welcomed as a friend. Shackleton could feel it creep up, very close, and intentionally needed to steer his will away from the tempting mercy it promised. He later said that the greatest sacrifice he made for his men was not his willingness to die for them, but his willingness to stay alive for them when death would have been "like a drink of sweet nectar." Shackleton knew the men stranded on Elephant Island had placed their trust in him, and he believed it was a cause worth being brave for.

After traveling long, arduous hours over peak after peak, the men came to the top of a raging waterfall within a few miles of the whaling station. They could not turn back, or they would die. There was simply no way for them to re-climb the peaks they just descended and choose another route between sheer cliffs of ice and darkened depths before food — and time — ran out. The three were left with no choice but to climb down through the roaring waters of the falls.

Shackleton's favorite poem, "Prospice," was penned by Robert Browning. Shackleton and his wife, Emily, used the word prospice frequently in letters and telegrams they exchanged with one another. The word means "look forward."

PROSPICE

When the snows begin, and the blasts denote
I am nearing the place,
The power of the night, the press of the storm,
The post of the foe;
Where he stands, the Arch Fear in a visible form,
Yet the strong man must go:
For the journey is done and the summit attained,
And the barriers fall...
I was ever a fighter, so – one fight more,
The best and the last!
I would hate that death bandaged my eyes, and forbore,
And bade me creep past.
No! let me taste the whole of it, fare like my peers
The heroes of old...
For sudden the worst turns the best to the brave,
The black minute's at end...

The men stared at the daunting waterfall before them. Then, they fastened their rope to a protrusion of ice at the top of it, making sure the blade would hold the weight of a man. One at a time, each of them slid down the rope, nearly drowning in the deluge of rushing current which poured over the falls and washed against their bodies with frigid force.

Once at the bottom, the men, soaked to the bone and shivering, lacked the time to celebrate. The drenched group trudged forcibly forward.

On the morning of May 20, the sufferers stood on a glacier, not far from the whaling station. It was almost 7:00 a.m., and the three eagerly awaited the sound of the station's steam whistle which blew faithfully at that time every morning. With clockwork precision it came, like sweet familiar music, sending chills up the spines of the men. This was the first sound of the outside world they had heard in more than seventeen months.

It was an affecting moment. Shackleton wrote, "It was hard to describe. Pain and aches, boat journey, marches, hunger and fatigue seemed to belong to the limbo of forgotten things, and there remained only the perfect contentment that comes from work accomplished."

Not long after, the half-dead men descended the final slope, staggering into the whaling camp, barely able to believe they had survived. Their faltering steps led them through the camp and to the door of Captain Thoralf Sorlle, manager of the station. Sorlle was one of the last men Shackleton spoke to before the expedition ventured south from the island and into the waters at the fringe of the world.

The men knocked. As Sorlle opened the door, he looked out at the "ragged, filthy and evil smelling" group, their identity hidden by their "long hair and beards, matted with soot and blubber." The three, numbed with cold, stood outside Sorlle's door peering in at him.

"Who the hell are you?" demanded Sorlle.

Shackleton responded, "Do you not know me?"

Sorlle, staring at him, paused and said very slowly, "I know your voice."

Then Shackleton "quietly" delivered the words, "My name is Shackleton."

Sorlle immediately turned his head and wept. He thought these men were dead. The whole world thought they were dead.

The following morning Shackleton, after a hot bath, wrote a letter to his wife, Emily, telling her of the ordeal the crew suffered. He included the sentence: "I have not had my clothes off since August 1, 1915."

Shackleton, determined to get his men to safety, organized an immediate rescue mission. A ship was offered by the Norwegian whalers at the camp to retrieve the three men on the other side of the island. A few of these volunteers were white-haired men, bent with age, their faces "lined and seamed by the storms of half a century." Every man at the whaling station eagerly offered his service to do whatever was necessary to save the stranded sailors in their hour of need. Sir Ernest explained it: "There is a brotherhood of the sea. The men who go down to the sea in ships, serving and suffering, fighting their endless battle against the caprice of wind and ocean, bring into their own horizons the perils and troubles of their brother sailormen."

Now that Shackleton had succeeded in uniting the six men who journeyed to South Georgia, he knew it was time to organize the rescue mission that would bring the other twenty-two men home who were still stranded on Elephant Island, waiting for his return.

The first of four attempted rescue missions over the next several months ensued. Due to the extreme buildup of ice floes surrounding Elephant Island—the effects of

The frozen kingdom

"Only explorers witness such sights."

C. Alexander

another Antarctic winter season—the first three attempts were unsuccessful, although one of these did come within sight of the island before it was forced to turn back by the ice. Finally, on August 30, 1916, nineteen months and twelve days since the *Endurance* became trapped in the ice, and over two full years since the ship originally left England, the *Yelcho*, a small steamer Shackleton borrowed for the rescue, weaved its way through the heavy ice to the grim shores of Elephant Island. The floes around the island had cleared a bit that day—and that day only. The clearing proved to be just enough room to allow passage between the floes in order to launch a lifeboat to deliver the twenty-two men from their icy captivity.

Five months prior, those same twenty-two had watched Shackleton and his five volunteers willingly embark into the stormy seas in the *James Caird*. As the *Caird* made its desperate crossing, and Sir Ernest led the three-man party through the South Georgia Mountains, the men on Elephant Island anxiously awaited the return of their leader.

The group, camped near the shore, lived beneath the two remaining lifeboats turned upside down (after their attempts to dig an ice cave for shelter failed). Canvas material from the tents was attached to the exterior, and four-foot stone walls were constructed in order to raise the boats higher. This crude shelter barely protected them against the unceasing wind and snow, nor provided comfort. (Twenty-two men were crammed "like sardines" under the two small boats which consisted of a total area of only 20 feet by 10 feet.)

The hut remained completely dark—all day, all night—except when a candle was lit to cook their meager food by, or when a man opened the small canvas door to venture out. It was the only light shed on the men cramped inside the dwelling.

In some ways it was better not to possess the ability to examine the conditions in which they survived. "The hut grows more grimy every day," observed one of the journals. "Everything is sooty black. It is at least comforting to feel that we can become no filthier."

The month of May brought awful weather and hurricane-like winds as winter approached. Powerful gusts rolled down the glaciers which loomed above them on the mountainsides, gaining speed as they traveled, and arriving suddenly at nearly 200 m.p.h., with the only warning being a sound like fast-approaching thunder. The experience of these winds was captured in the following journal entry: "Leonard Hussey was outside in the blizzard digging up the day's meat, which had frozen to the ground, when a gust caught him and drove him down towards the sea. Fortunately, when he reached the softer sand, he managed to stick his pick into the ground and hold on with both hands till the squall had passed."

Frank Wild, leader of the men, continuously filled the group with hope and was ever-positive in his thinking. Every day, through more than four months of waiting, having no possible way of knowing what fate was in store for them, Wild would rise in

Attempting to dig a sheltering cave on Elephant Island

"One curious feature noted in this blizzard was the fact that huge sheets of ice as big as windowpanes, and about a quarter of an inch thick, were being hurled about by the wind, making it as dangerous to walk about outside as if one were in an avalanche of splintered glass."

Sir Ernest Shackleton

59

Saved - at long last!
August 30, 1916

"It was just before lunchtime that George Marston, who was standing outside, saw a ship emerging from the mist that hung over the sea... At first when Marston yelled 'Ship O!' we took no notice, mistaking it for the much more customary call of 'Lunch O!' It was not long, however, before he came running up towards the hut, breathless and excited. In a state of great excitement, he gasped, 'There's a ship!'... We made a dive through the narrow door of the hut... We were so excited and thrilled by the news that some of us tore down the canvas walls to get out and see the great sight. Then... the ship stopped. A boat was lowered. And we were able to recognize Shackleton as he got into it. Again we gave a cheer, with more feelings from the heart than I could express in words."

Leonard Hussey

the morning and announce to the struggling group, "Roll up your sleeping bags, boys! The Boss may come today."

Month after month of strife and near-starvation dragged on until the miracle day, August 30, 1916. A ship was spotted on the horizon, growing larger as it approached. The men shouted and cheered in crazed excitement, straining their eyes to see the too-good-to-be-true sight.

As the rescue vessel approached the celebratory shores of Elephant Island, Shackleton was overcome with anxiety. He feared that not all of the men had survived another Antarctic winter over the past five months. Leaning over the side of the boat, peering through a pair of binoculars, he scanned the wind-swept beach. Nervously, he mumbled to Captain Worsley, who stood beside him, "There are only two, Skipper." Then, "No, four!" He paused, then continued excitedly, "I see six—eight—" and finally, "They are all there! Every one of them! They are all saved!" Shackleton was instantly filled with the calm of relief, and the gratification that only heroes know.

Drawing closer to the icy shore, he called to Wild in a voice to be heard above all others, "Is everyone well?" Wild returned his question, "All safe! All well!" The long trial of mind and body had come to an end. They were saved. Every man survived.

Shackleton was fond of saying that the highest compliment ever paid to him during his life came from the men on Elephant Island who greeted him on the beach with the words, "We knew you'd come."

Epilogue

In an age when exploration and discovery captivated the public during the late 1800's and early 1900's, twenty-eight courageous men made an attempt to cross the continent of Antarctica on foot. Their story lives on today as an extraordinary example of perseverance against all odds.

As remarkable as the feats within this story are, it is doubtful they could have been accomplished without the unwavering optimism of Sir Ernest Shackleton who repeatedly applied the principle of positive thinking to overcome the persistent impossibilities which challenged him and his men daily. Shackleton's "invincible optimism," as was observed by crewmember Peter Wordie, who served on board the *Endurance*, was permanently bound to the success of the story.

"His unfailing cheeriness means a lot," wrote another crewmember, Thomas Orde-Lees. "He is one of the greatest optimists I have ever known." Orde-Lees then added, "To serve such a leader is one of the greatest pleasures of the whole trip."

Shackleton displayed the outstanding characteristic of putting the needs of those he led to the forefront of his thoughts. He understood the importance of this, as every great commander does. Shackleton never took advantage of the preferential amenities that were rightfully his as leader of the expedition. Crewmember Lionel Greenstreet observed, "He didn't care if he went without a shirt on his own back, so long as the men he was leading had sufficient clothing."

Shackleton gave his mittens away to a comrade when he noticed the poor fellow's pair fall overboard during a seven-day boat journey to Elephant Island. He also made the decision to sleep in the lowest quality woolen bag when he and his men camped for five long months on the ice. Shackleton, to preserve the morale of his group, always knew what needed to be done—and when to do it.

Sir Ernest took a very lenient stand on disciplinary actions, as well. He stressed equality and also, as crewmember Leonard Hussey wrote of it, "was quite willing to overlook the bad, and just remember the good in everyone." By choosing to downplay mistakes, and embrace achievements instead, Shackleton was able to bring out the best in his men, earning him their trust and respect.

Ernest Shackleton used another unique style of leadership which was far before his time. Rather than exuding himself as a figure of domination, he wanted his men to see him as one of the group. So, he broke down the traditional hierarchies of status among ranks in the party. Scientists and officers helped the low-ranking sailors with grudge work, and these deck-hands then assisted the scientists. No man was given preferential treatment over another, including Sir Ernest himself. Shackleton made an effort to partake in even the most menial chores, and set an example by completing these tasks to perfection.

Shackleton intentionally chose to lead his men by example instead of authority. In so doing, he taught his crew how to employ their thoughts to overcome obstacles met along the way. Sir Ernest challenged the men to distance their minds from the suffering at hand by combining the unpleasant situation with a bit of imagination, the end result being a tolerance for circumstances which would have otherwise eroded them physically and mentally. Once, while the men stood stranded in biting winds, watching their comrades race dogsleds around a track of snow, imaginary ice-cream cones were dispensed among the crowd, to much amusement. The group simply convinced their minds that the situation was better than it was, and in so doing, it became not only tolerable, but at times, quite pleasant. On another occasion the men pretended they were on a picnic while dining on their near-starvation rations.

"It has been a lovely day," wrote Dr. Macklin in his journal after the ship was crushed, "and it is hard to think that we are in a frightfully precarious situation." Crewmember Lionel Greenstreet noted shortly thereafter, "It is one of the finest days we ever had, and it is a pleasure to be alive." Both diary entries are examples of how the men overcame the suffering of the physical realm with the mental virtues of hope and perception.

Although the trials seemed unending, Shackleton's concentrated and unwavering focus could lift him above the desperate conditions surrounding any situation. He seemed to be in possession of an uncanny ability to beat back adversity by simply believing he could. "Dame Fortune, Sir Ernest's old and constant friend," wrote crewmember Thomas Orde-Lees in his journal, "again favored us." (It hardly seems possible that the crew aboard the *Endurance* could look upon the fates as having been kind to them after the immense scope of adversity they endured is understood, but narrow escapes from death were a constant theme throughout the details of the adventure.)

A leader among leaders, Commander Shackleton taught his men how to concentrate intentionally on victory. He refused to allow even the possibility of failure to enter his thinking. Success was the only option Shackleton would entertain, and if there wasn't a way, he would make one.

Bibliography

South by Sir Ernest Shackleton, 1919, Heinemann.
Shackleton: A Memory by Harold Begbie, 1922, Mills and Boon
The Life of Sir Ernest Shackleton by Hugh Robert Mill, 1923, William Heinemann Ltd.
Shackleton's Last Voyage by Frank Wild, 1923, Cassell and Company
Endurance by Frank Worsley, 1931, Philip Allen.
Shackleton's Boat Journey by Frank Worsley, London, Philip Allan, n.d.
Argonauts of the South by Frank Hurley, 1925, G.P. Putnam's Sons
Shackleton's Argonauts by Frank Hurley, 1948, Angus and Robertson
South With Shackleton by Leonard Hussey, 1949, Sampson Low
The American on the Endurance by William L. Bakewell, 2003, Dukes Hall Publishing
Shackleton by Margery and James Fisher, 1957, James Barrie Books Ltd.
Endurance by Alfred Lansing, 1959, McGraw-Hill Book Company
Men of the Antarctic by Gerald Bowman, 1959, Fleet Publishing
The Ross Sea Shore Party 1914-1917 by R.W. Richards, 1962, SPRI
Shackleton's Voyage by Donald Chidsey, 1967, Tandem Books
Antarctica: The Last Continent by Ian Cameron, 1974, Little, Brown & Company
Shackleton's Forgotten Argonauts by Lennard Bickel, 1982, Macmillan
Antarctica: Great Stories from the Frozen Continent, 1985, Reader's Digest Books
Shackleton by Roland Huntford, 1986, Atheneum
North Pole, South Pole by Bertrand Imbert, 1992, Harry N. Abrams, Inc.
Shackleton's Boat by Harding Dunnett, 1996, Neville & Harding
Mrs. Chippy's Last Expedition by Caroline Alexander, 1997, Bloomsbury Publishing
Shipwreck at the Bottom of the World by Jennifer Armstrong, 1998, Crown Publishers
Shackleton's Captain by John Bell Thomsen, 1998, Hazard Press
Ice Story by Elizabeth Cody Kimmel, 1999, Clarion Books
The Endurance by Caroline Alexander, 1999, Alfred A. Knopf, Inc.
Leading at the Edge by Dennis Perkins, 2000, Amacon
Shackleton's Way by Margo Morrell and Stephanie Capparell, 2001, Viking Penguin
South With Endurance, 2001, Book Creation Ltd. London
To the Ends of the Earth by Richard Sale, 2002, Harper Collins

In addition, previously published entries from crewmember diaries, newspaper articles, magazine articles and video documentaries were used in our research.